Dear Parents and Educators,

Welcome to Penguin Young Readers! As parents and educators, you know that each child develops at his or her own pace—in terms of speech, critical thinking, and, of course, reading. Penguin Young Readers recognizes this fact. As a result, each Penguin Young Readers book is assigned a traditional easy-to-read level (1–4) as well as a Guided Reading Level (A–P). Both of these systems will help you choose the right book for your child. Please refer to the back of each book for specific leveling information. Penguin Young Readers features esteemed authors and illustrators, stories about favorite characters, fascinating nonfiction, and more!

Pink Snow and Other Weird Weather

LEVEL **3**

GUIDED READING LEVEL **K**

This book is perfect for a **Transitional Reader** who:
- can read multisyllable and compound words;
- can read words with prefixes and suffixes;
- is able to identify story elements (beginning, middle, end, plot, setting, characters, problem, solution); and
- can understand different points of view.

Here are some **activities** you can do during and after reading this book:
- Nonfiction: Nonfiction books deal with facts and events that are real. Talk about the elements of nonfiction. Then make a list of what you learned in this book about *really* weird weather. For example, you now know that lightning hits the Empire State Building in New York about 40 times per year.
- Compound Words: A compound word is made when two words are joined together to form a new word. *Snowflakes* is a compound word that is used in this story. Reread the story and try to find other compound words.

Remember, sharing the love of reading with a child is the best gift you can give!

—Bonnie Bader, EdM
  Penguin Young Readers program

*Penguin Young Readers are leveled by independent reviewers applying the standards developed by Irene Fountas and Gay Su Pinnell in *Matching Books to Readers: Using Leveled Books in Guided Reading*, Heinemann, 1999.

To Chris—JD

To Joan Farabee, Vickie Geckle, and
Gayle Reichert—cool teachers all—
and to Jackie, our black cat
(See if you can find him!)—HP

Special thanks to Brendon Hoch, the
Lamont-Doherty Earth Observatory.

Penguin Young Readers
Published by the Penguin Group
Penguin Group (USA) Inc., 375 Hudson Street, New York, New York 10014, USA
Penguin Group (Canada), 90 Eglinton Avenue East, Suite 700, Toronto, Ontario M4P 2Y3, Canada
(a division of Pearson Penguin Canada Inc.)
Penguin Books Ltd., 80 Strand, London WC2R 0RL, England
Penguin Group Ireland, 25 St. Stephen's Green, Dublin 2, Ireland (a division of Penguin Books Ltd.)
Penguin Group (Australia), 250 Camberwell Road, Camberwell, Victoria 3124, Australia
(a division of Pearson Australia Group Pty. Ltd.)
Penguin Books India Pvt. Ltd., 11 Community Centre, Panchsheel Park, New Delhi—110 017, India
Penguin Group (NZ), 67 Apollo Drive, Rosedale, Auckland 0632, New Zealand
(a division of Pearson New Zealand Ltd.)
Penguin Books (South Africa) (Pty.) Ltd., 24 Sturdee Avenue,
Rosebank, Johannesburg 2196, South Africa

Penguin Books Ltd., Registered Offices: 80 Strand, London WC2R 0RL, England

Library of Congress Control Number: 98014336

ISBN 978-0-448-41858-2   10 9 8 7 6 5 4 3 2 1

PINK SNOW
and Other Weird Weather

by Jennifer Dussling
illustrated by Heidi Petach

Penguin Young Readers
An Imprint of Penguin Group (USA) Inc.

You are outside playing.

And it starts to snow.

Yippee!

But wait!

There is something strange

about this snow.

It is dark pink!

Pink snow?

Is that possible?

Yes!

Snow is not always white.

Every once in a while

snow can be a different color.

How does this happen?

Snow is made in clouds.

Sometimes strong winds

pick up tiny bits

of red soil and dust.

These bits of soil are blown

up into snow clouds.

Snow forms around red soil.

The snow looks dark pink!

Most people never see pink snow.

It is very rare.

It is very weird.

But sometimes the weather
does very weird things.

It is very hot
when it should be cold.

Or very cold

when it should be hot.

Or strange things rain down from the sky.

Here is what happened
one day in France in 1833.
Rain was falling on the streets
of a small town outside Paris.
People rushed from place to
place with their umbrellas.

Then all of a sudden,
something else started
to fall with the rain.
Toads.
Toads were falling from the sky!
They dropped on the rooftops.
They hit umbrellas.
Then they hopped around
in the wet streets!

The people of the town

must have been amazed.

And maybe they were afraid.

How did this happen?

Scientists think there is a simple answer.

Sometimes a special kind of storm

forms over an ocean or a lake.

It is called a waterspout.

The strong winds of a waterspout
whirl around and around.
A waterspout can suck up water.
It can suck up frogs or fish, too.

Sometimes the waterspout

will move over dry land.

When it starts to die out,

the frogs or fish fall to the ground.

In 1894, it rained jellyfish
in England.

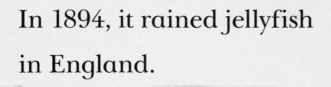

Other places have had snails, worms,
or even snakes fall from the sky.

Like a waterspout, a tornado is a storm
with fierce winds that whirl around.
Tornadoes are weird.
They move in crazy paths.

A tornado can crush one house
and leave the next one alone.

It can strip the bark off a tree
or pluck the feathers off a chicken.

In 1974, a tornado in Ohio
knocked down a farmhouse.
Everything inside was broken—
beds, chairs, tables.
Only three things were not broken.
A mirror, a case of eggs, and a box
of Christmas tree ornaments!

The unlucky town of Codell, Kansas, is almost like a magnet for tornadoes. A tornado hit Codell in 1916. In 1917, a tornado hit Codell. Again in 1918, a tornado hit Codell.

And here is the strangest thing:
The tornado struck each year on
May 20—the same exact day!

Some people say lightning never
strikes the same place twice.
That is not true.
Lightning hits the
Empire State Building in New York City
about 40 times a year.
So what, you say?
A building cannot get hurt
by lightning.
But did you know one man was struck
by lightning seven times?

His name was Roy Sullivan,

and he was a park ranger.

One time he was fishing.

One time he was driving a truck.

One time he was in his front yard.

And one time he was even inside!

Lightning melted his watch.

It burned his hair.

But it didn't kill him.

Scientists don't know why Roy
Sullivan was hit so many times.
Lightning is just a bolt of electricity.
It can jump from a cloud
to the ground.
It can jump from the ground
to a cloud.
Lightning can even jump
from cloud to cloud.

Once a gas station worker
saw lightning hit a flock of
pelicans flying through the air.
It killed all 27 of them!

That's just plain weird.
Here are some more
weird weather facts.
You may not believe them.
But they are all true!
In Montana in 1887,
the biggest snowflakes ever
fell from the sky.
Each one was 15 inches across—
as big as a dinner plate!

In Hawaii,

there is one mountain

where it rains about 350 days a year!

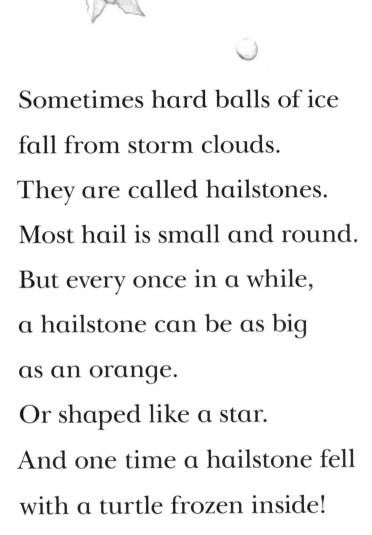

Sometimes hard balls of ice

fall from storm clouds.

They are called hailstones.

Most hail is small and round.

But every once in a while,

a hailstone can be as big

as an orange.

Or shaped like a star.

And one time a hailstone fell

with a turtle frozen inside!

Then there is the story of 1816.

The weather that year

was very, very weird.

In Europe and in parts of America,

1816 is known as

"The Year Without a Summer."

And it was all caused by a volcano.

It's true.

In April 1815,

a volcano erupted on an island

in the Pacific Ocean.

The volcano spewed

lots and lots of ash and dust

into the air.

People on nearby islands did not see
the sun for three whole days.
The ash and dust from the volcano
stayed in the air above the earth.
Then it drifted over other countries—
ones far away from the volcano.
It blocked out the heat from the sun.
It caused a cold spell.

Even a year later,
parts of New England
got six inches of snow . . .
in June!
There were bad frosts all summer long.
Crops died.

In Virginia,

Thomas Jefferson

had such a bad harvest on his farm,

he finally had to ask for a loan!

Most of the time

you don't even think about weather.

It is sunny or rainy.

Hot or cold.

But sometimes,

you can't help but notice it!

So next time it rains, watch out!

Who knows?

Maybe a frog will fall on your head!